ELIZABETH VISITS *the* ABBEY

Published by :

 Clear Faith Publishing
781 Caxambas Drive
Marco Island, FL 34145

Copyright © 2022 Phyllis Zagano

All Rights Reserved. No part of this book may be used or reproduced in any manner whatsoever, whether electronic, mechanical, photocopying, recording or otherwise, without the prior written permission of the publisher.

ISBN: 978-1-940414-38-6
Cover & Interior Design by Doug Cordes
Cover photography by Valerie O'Sullivan
Photography compliments Glencairn Abbey, Co. Waterford, Ireland

The mission of Clear Faith Publishing is to spread joy, peace, and comfort through great writing about spirituality, religion, and faith that touches the reader and serves those who live on the margins. Portions of the proceeds from this book are donated to organizations that feed, shelter, and provide counsel for those in need.

For more information, please visit us at:
www.clearfaithpublishing.com

Elizabeth Visits the Abbey

PHYLLIS ZAGANO

For Elizabeths everywhere.
May your dreams come true.

CONTENTS

PROLOGUE	ix
ONE	1
TWO	3
THREE	5
FOUR	9
FIVE	13
SIX	15
SEVEN	17
EIGHT	19
NINE	21
TEN	25
ELEVEN	29
TWELVE	33
THIRTEEN	37
FOURTEEN	41
FIFTEEN	45
SIXTEEN	49
SEVENTEEN	53
EIGHTEEN	57
NINETEEN	61
TWENTY	63
TWENTY-ONE	67
TWENTY-TWO	71
TWENTY-THREE	75
TWENTY-FOUR	77
TWENTY-FIVE	79
TWENTY-SIX	81

PROLOGUE

It gives me great pleasure to introduce the reader of this book to Elizabeth, the beloved daughter of Meg and Bill. Elizabeth is in the sixth grade at St. Joseph's School in one of the beautiful upper counties of New York, in an area called the Hudson Valley region.

St. Joseph's is the same school Elizabeth's big brother, Bill Jr., and her big sister, Nancy, attended. Today, Bill Jr. is a senior at Georgetown University, in Washington, DC, and Nancy is a sophomore at Loyola University, in Baltimore.

Elizabeth's parents very much wanted to bring Elizabeth to Ireland, where they first met each other and fell in love some twenty-five years ago.

But first, this is how Meg and Bill met.

Bill was an American in the textile business, and he was on a business trip to find out more about dry goods manufactured in England, Ireland, Scotland, and Wales. It was his first trip overseas for the company, and he used Dublin, the capital of the Republic of Ireland, as his European base. From Dublin, Bill would fly to London in England, then went by train to Glasgow in Scotland, then again by train to Cardiff in Wales, before flying back to Dublin. Then, he drove up to Derry in Northern Ireland for a few days. Then, back again to Dublin.

Bill always returned to the big Shelbourne Hotel near St. Stephen's Green in Dublin. The Shelbourne was—and still is—a very expensive hotel, more expensive than any hotel Bill had ever stayed in. But Bill's company had a contract with the hotel for one of the small rooms in the back, so he stayed there whenever he was in Dublin.

In the front of the hotel, just to the left of the lobby, Bill could get a sandwich and sit by the big fireplace in a tiny bar just about any time of the day or night. He liked the sitting area by the fireplace, with its small coffee table and big, comfortable chairs. So, whenever Bill was not meeting clients, or walking around Dublin, or sleeping, he was usually in the bar, by the fireplace, and in a big chair.

It was right there in the Shelbourne Bar that Bill met Meg.

CHAPTER ONE

Meg was beautiful. Bill had never seen such a beautiful woman in his life. She had long, black hair and big blue eyes that won his heart long before he ever spoke to her. Meg served the people in the bar seating area, bringing them their sandwiches and drinks, or maybe tea and scones, depending on the time of day.

Meg was also a student. She studied art and design at an academy not far from the Shelbourne Hotel, in fact, just across St. Stephen's Green. They call it "Stephen's Green" in Dublin. It is twenty-two acres of parkland with beautiful plantings: shrubs and trees and flowers. Often, Meg walked through Stephen's Green on her way to or from school, depending on when her classes met and when she had to work.

Bill never knew when Meg would be in the Shelbourne Bar, but he was really determined to meet her. One day, he followed her when she left work. As it happened, Meg lived in another direction from her school, up on Baggot Street with the Sisters of Mercy. The building is a big house called the Mercy International Center, and it is where Catherine McAuley began the Sisters of Mercy. Bill stopped across the street when Meg went through the big red doors. He stood and watched the doors close and saw the big statue of Catherine McAuley in a nun's habit, standing with a young girl in front of the building. It was a very welcoming scene, but not for him.

Bill was afraid Meg was a nun!

As it turned out, Meg thought she might like to become a nun, like her big sister Marie.

Meg and Marie and their brother, Jimmy, grew up outside Cork, the second largest city in Ireland, about three hours (depending on the traffic) southwest of Dublin. All three were very close in age, and very, very close friends as well as siblings. When Marie left to join the convent—actually, it was the Cistercian Abbey in West Cork—all three cried the whole night before, because they thought they would never be together again.

Now, Meg was in art school, working at the Shelbourne Hotel and living with the Sisters of Mercy, and Jimmy was in the Irish Naval Service over at Haulbowline, just across Cork Harbor from where they grew up, and Marie was a cloistered nun at St. Joseph's Abbey in West Cork.

CHAPTER TWO

In Dublin, Bill did not give up on Meg. His company often let him choose the cities he would visit, so whenever he could, he planned a northern European trip. He always made sure his first and last stop was in Dublin. And, he always stayed at the Shelbourne Hotel.

About a year after Bill first saw Meg, he was in the hotel bar (as usual, by the fireplace) eating a sandwich. It was too early for lunch, but he had just arrived from New York and for some reason his hotel room was not ready. Bill was very tired, so he ordered tea with his meal instead of his usual glass of water. Meg brought the pot of tea, a cup and a saucer, and a cloth dinner napkin (it's called a "serviette" in Ireland) and set them on the coffee table. Then, Meg brought the sandwich plate as Bill was pouring his tea.

But just as Meg bent to put the plate upon the table, she bumped Bill's arm, and he poured the tea all over the coffee table, and even got some on his pants. What a mess! We will never know whether Bill or Meg was more embarrassed. They both turned a little red in the face. Bill stood up and brushed his pants with the table napkin and Meg bent to wipe the coffee table. They were standing very close together.

Suddenly, Bill burst out laughing. He was very jet-lagged and felt a little silly. Maybe because he was tired or because he was embarrassed, he touched Meg's arm and said, half-laughing but quite seriously: "That's no big deal, don't worry about it." Meg was still embarrassed. She apologized to Bill over and over again. Bill kept saying, "Don't worry about it."

Suddenly, they realized they were both talking at the same time, and they laughed. Bill decided this was his chance. He introduced himself.

Meg was actually very happy that this tall, handsome stranger was back at the Shelbourne. She had thought about him over the months when he was not there. She remembered how once, maybe a year ago, he seemed to follow her back to the Mercy International Center.

She said, "My name is Meg."

"I'm Bill," he said.

They looked at each other for a long time. Then Meg went back to work, and Bill went back to his sandwich. Soon, Bill's room was ready, and he went up to take a nap.

CHAPTER THREE

When Bill came down from his room, at about 5:00 that evening, Meg was just leaving work. Bill saw her and asked if he could walk her home. He already knew where she lived, and Meg already knew he knew where she lived, so off they went up Baggot Street to the Mercy International Center. They stopped in front of the big, red doors, next to the statue of Catherine McAuley. Bill said: "Maybe we could have lunch tomorrow, or supper?"

And so, the next day they shared an evening meal, and the next day after that. Bill was in Dublin a lot that year, and on every trip, he extended his stay a little longer. Meg and Bill became very good friends, and one day, when they were walking through Stephen's Green, Bill asked Meg if she would be his wife.

It was a big question, and a big decision for Meg. After all, Bill was an American and Meg was an Irish woman. The United States was very far from Dublin. She was almost finished with school, but America was also very, very far from Cork and Jimmy and Marie and their parents.

She said yes.

The wedding was in Cork City, at the South Presentation Convent where Meg had gone to school. In 1775, a Cork woman named Nano Nagle (her real name was Honora) founded the Presentation Sisters—their full name is the Sisters of the Presentation of the Blessed Virgin Mary—to educate the poor in Cork. Nano was one of the few Catholic Irish girls to get an education in the late eighteenth century. There was a law against Catholic schools in Ireland then, and it was also against the law to leave Ireland for Catholic school abroad. But, because Nano's father was a merchant, she and her sister Anne were able to go to a Catholic school in Paris.

So, back to Meg and Bill. Their wedding was lovely. Jimmy was there, but not Marie because her abbey was cloistered. That meant the nuns could not leave the abbey property except for doctor and dentist appointments. Meg missed having her big sister at the wedding, but she understood the rules. After the ceremony and the reception (out at the Blarney Woollen Mill), Jimmy drove Meg and Bill out to Marie's abbey in Magarry.

St. Joseph's Cistercian Abbey, Magarry, was an imposing place. The big electric gates swung open when Jimmy spoke into the little sound box on the driver's side of the car. They drove to the front entrance and rang the bell, and a short nun opened the door. They were expected, so they all went inside. Meg was no longer in her wedding gown, having changed into her traveling clothes, and Bill had traded his formal suit for something more comfortable. Only Jimmy, who was in the wedding party, was still dressed up.

Marie came to the parlor. She was so happy to see them, and they were so happy to see her. Marie was tall, as tall as Meg, with the same dark hair and big blue eyes. She was in her every-day habit (the nuns kept a nicer one for Sundays and holidays), and they could see her hair a little because her veil only started where a headband might. It was an interesting habit: a long white dress with a black tunic over it, all tied around her waist with a leather belt. Marie wore clunky black shoes and white socks, and she was certainly not as stylish as Meg in her pink going-away outfit.

The two sisters hugged and cried and hugged and cried again, but too soon it was time for Marie to go to prayers and for Meg and Bill to go off on their honeymoon. It would be a long time before they saw each other again, because Meg and Bill were moving to the United States.

CHAPTER FOUR

In fact, it was a very long time before the three of them were together again. Meg and Bill began their married life in a little cottage on an estate in Westchester County, about an hour north of New York City. Bill took the train to work every day from Tarrytown, and he was very happy to do so. The train ride (on an express train) took only about thirty minutes. Then he was in Grand Central Station, at 42nd Street, and he only had to walk a few blocks south to his office.

That, of course, was when Bill was in the US. He still had the same job at the same company as when he met Meg. He did not make so many trips to Ireland now, because so much of the business had moved to different countries, like China and El Salvador. So, when he went on a trip, it was either very long (to China) or a little shorter (to El Salvador) than his two-week trips to Ireland and the rest of Europe.

Over the years, Meg and Bill did make a few trips to Ireland, and they always managed to get out to Magarry in West Cork to see Marie at the abbey. But the timing never quite worked out so that Jimmy, who was still in the Irish Naval Service, could go out there with them.

Meanwhile, Meg and Bill enlarged their little family. First came Bill Jr., a bundle of energy with his mother's big blue eyes and his father's blond hair. Two years later, Nancy arrived. Just like Bill Jr., Nancy had big blue eyes and blonde hair. She was the prettiest little girl you ever saw, and she was just as energetic (and noisy) as her big brother, Bill Jr.

When Nancy and Bill Jr. were ten and twelve, about the same age Elizabeth is now, Meg and Bill took them to Ireland for a long vacation. Meg's brother, Uncle Jimmy, took them out to Haulbowline to see the big ship he worked on. Another day, he took them in a little chug-chug boat off the Old Head of Kinsale, near where the British ship RMS Lusitania sank during World War I. Uncle Jimmy told Bill Jr. and Nancy all sorts of things, like "Lusitania" is the old name for Portugal, and the sinking of the liner really is what got the United States into the war, and how people from the ship were rescued right where they were fishing now.

It was a wonderful and a very long day for twelve-year-old Bill Jr. and ten-year-old Nancy. They both came back home with lots of mackerel fish and a little bit of a sunburn.

The rest of the family vacation flew by. One day, Meg and Bill and Nancy and Bill Jr. took a two-hour bus ride up to Limerick from Cork and walked around the city. They went to the outdoor market—it's called the Milk Market—and they bought breads and cheeses and fruit for a little picnic that they took over to Arthur's Quay Park, on the River Shannon. Then they went into the Hunt Museum and saw all the beautiful things there. In a special room, they saw rosary beads made of amber and of silver and of wood. There was a funny looking carved piece called the "Beverly Crozier," and Meg explained to the children that it was put on the top of a stick the bishop carried as a symbol of his high office. It was carved from walrus ivory, the ivory from a walrus tusk. Both Bill Jr. and Nancy were surprised to learn that walruses had tusks.

There were bells and crosses and maces and chalices and more crosses. There was a little bronze box called a reliquary box, and Meg explained that it was for relics, but she did not go into detail about what that meant. There was a big pointed hat that Meg said was called a miter, and it had gold and precious stones on it. Meg said the bishop wore it when he was doing official things. There were gold rings and stone rings, but Meg could not find a bishop's ring, and so she just told the children that he had one and it was a sign of his authority.

Bill missed the religious education lecture. He was looking at all the different textiles. There were tapestries from the fifteenth century, like carpets with pictures woven in them to hang up on the wall. There were beautiful dresses and evening gowns and he loved the names of their colors: "pink ice" and "blue hyacinth."

The four met up again just as Bill was admiring a red and white brocade cope, the kind a bishop would wear when he was doing something official in his cathedral but not saying Mass.

There was so much to see, but it was getting late and they had to go over to the Limerick Bus Station to get the bus back to Cork. They walked up the main street and to the station. They waited in the line, and then boarded the bus.

Bill and Bill Jr. and Nancy fell asleep almost immediately, but Meg did not. She wanted to drink in every minute of every day in Ireland, because she did not know when she would return. The bus turned out of the station and onto the road, out behind the stores and the hospital, and soon headed straight down to Cork. Meg saw the little towns as they passed. Sometimes, the bus would stop to pick up another traveler. Sometimes, it would stop to let someone off.

Meg saw the hills with sheep sleeping in little groups. She saw the fields with horses or cows standing around. She wanted to wake Nancy, snuggled beside her, but she did not. Bill and Bill Jr. were across the aisle, sound asleep, so Meg was left with her own thoughts. She wondered if she would see the sky, the trees, the hedgerows, and the little ponds ever again. She wondered what the future would bring. Would she have another baby?

Then Meg saw a magpie. Then she saw another. Then she saw a third! Good luck! The magpie meant Meg would indeed come back to Ireland. She remembered the old nursery rhyme about magpies: "One for Sorrow, Two for Joy, Three for a Girl, Four for a Boy...." And then she fell asleep.

CHAPTER FIVE

In fact, Meg did have another baby, and ("Three for a Girl") it was a girl! Meg and Bill named their new baby girl Elizabeth.

Elizabeth was so much younger than her older brother and sister that it was almost like being an only child. She was so pretty, with big blue eyes and dark hair. "A real Irish beauty," Bill said when they brought the baby home from the hospital. Of course, Nancy and Bill Jr. were excited to meet their little sister, who grew up in their shadows and who laughed as much as they did.

Elizabeth grew to be a very studious little girl. She loved her mother's stories about growing up in Ireland, and she had a map of Ireland on the bulletin board in her little bedroom. It seemed like a magical place to Elizabeth, where all sorts of dreams could come true.

Once, Meg told Elizabeth a story about how she and one of Meg's friends got into so much trouble at the South Presentation Convent, where they went to school. The sisters there were doing some renovations to Nano Nagle's grave. Meg bent over to have a look in the opening and some coins, she thinks they were a few pennies and a farthing, fell out of her pocket and onto the coffin. The two girls giggled loudly. They were half-frightened and half-laughing as they tried to reach into the open gravesite, trying to collect the coins.

Suddenly, the mother superior appeared behind them.

Sister Mary Francis of the Assumption was a formidable woman, at least six feet tall in her long black habit. Her coif (a headdress with a long black veil) seemed to make Sister a few inches taller.

"Ladies," her stern voice boomed out, "what exactly did you have in mind?"

The two girls turned, red-faced and, at least the way Meg tells it now, empty handed. The coins were lost and so was their secret. They were not about to tell Sister Mary Francis of the Assumption that Meg lost money in Nano Nagle's grave!

Meg told Elizabeth many stories about growing up in Ireland. She spoke about how she and her sister, Elizabeth's Auntie Marie, and their parents would go out to Haulbowline to visit Uncle Jimmy when he first joined the Irish Naval Service, and how they would go fishing in Cork Harbor, and how they once went out, off the Old Head of Kinsale, near where the survivors (and the dead people) from the Lusitania tragedy were brought to shore. They caught a lot of mackerel that day.

Meg told Elizabeth of the golden summer evenings in Ireland and the brilliant colors on the trees and bushes in the fall. She told Elizabeth about the November rains and about the time the road down toward Crosshaven almost got washed into Cork Harbor.

Meg told Elizabeth about the spring, when magpies come alive and bounce all over the roads and hedgerows. And she told Elizabeth about the last time she was in Ireland, and when she and Elizabeth's dad and Nancy and Bill Jr. took a trip to Limerick on the bus, and how she saw three magpies on the ride home.

CHAPTER SIX

Elizabeth grew up loving Ireland and all things Irish. When she was in the fourth grade, there at St. Joseph's School, she wrote a homework assignment about St. Brigid, who lived in the sixth century. She wrote about how Brigid performed miracles and how she was ordained a bishop by Bishop Mel, even though there are many writers who do not want to believe that and even more who say Brigid never existed at all.

Elizabeth's favorite miracle was about how Brigid turned water into beer, but her teacher did not think that was the best part of the essay.

Brigid was head of a double monastery of monks and nuns and ruled them well and fairly. Her relics were destroyed during the sixteenth century, excepting some that rest in Lisbon, Portugal to this day. On St. Brigid's feast day, February 1, people in Ireland make a *Crosóg Bríde* (that's Irish for a Brigid Cross) and put it over their doorway to protect their home from harm.

But, to pick up the story where we began, we can now fast-forward to when Elizabeth's parents—Meg and Bill—very much wanted to bring Elizabeth to Ireland, where they first met each other and fell in love some twenty-five years before.

As it happened, Elizabeth's Easter vacation from St. Joseph's School was the same week (the week after Easter) that Bill had to make another business trip to Ireland. Both Bill Jr. and

Nancy were home for Easter, but they went back to college on Easter Monday. Meg and Bill and Elizabeth went out to Kennedy Airport that afternoon.

Of course, they were flying on *Aer Lingus*—Irish Airlines. For Elizabeth, this would be her first long airplane trip. She went once from Westchester Airport to Washington, DC with Meg and Bill to see Bill Jr. in a play at Georgetown (Nancy took the train down from Baltimore), but that was just a little plane. The plane to Ireland was so big, Elizabeth could not believe it. There were two aisles going up and down, two seats by each of the windows, and then four seats in the middle. They found their seats about halfway down in the middle, and it turned out that there was an empty seat in the row. The plane took off into the sunset, and Elizabeth could see the golden rays turn pink and orange and red, before they turned around and headed east, toward Ireland.

The cabin crew served supper and soon Elizabeth was fast asleep, curled up on the two middle seats, with her head on her mother's lap. She woke only when she saw some red light coming in from the window across the way, then pink and orange, and finally golden sunlight began to flood the cabin. It did not seem time for breakfast already, but Elizabeth sat up and drank the juice from the little plastic cup (her father helped her get the foil top off) and ate a delicious blueberry muffin.

CHAPTER SEVEN

Before she knew it, Elizabeth was standing in the customs and immigration line between her parents, who showed their passports to the lady in the booth. Elizabeth and her dad had blue US passports; her mom had a cranberry-colored European Union one from Ireland.

Then they collected their luggage, and just as soon as they got outside, they saw Uncle Jimmy, waving wildly. He had not seen Meg in so many years, and he had never met his "new" niece Elizabeth. The four of them piled into Uncle Jimmy's car, and off they went. Years ago, they could only take the small road, through Limerick and then south, but now there was a big motorway almost to Cork. It only took two hours now to get from Shannon Airport all the way home, and that included a stop to just walk around a bit and so Bill could get a cup of coffee.

They arrived, finally, Elizabeth thought, in front of a big Victorian house near the water, south of Cork. It was a bed 'n' breakfast that friends of Uncle Jimmy ran. The room was the biggest bedroom Elizabeth had ever seen! It overlooked the water and had its own bathroom (they called in *"en suite"*), and there was a little alcove on the other side of the bathroom with a small bed for Elizabeth.

The next few days sped by. Bill had some business meetings in Cork City and one up in Mallow, not more than an hour away. The next day, Uncle Jimmy drove them all to Cork City so Bill could go up to Dublin on the train, and Meg and Elizabeth and Uncle Jimmy spent the rest of the morning looking at shops and then had lunch over at the Crawford Art Gallery.

At the Crawford, Meg noticed one painting she remembered from when she was a little girl, called *Sunshine in the Beguinage*. A Beguinage, Meg told Elizabeth, was usually a group of little houses were ladies lived and worked. It was not exactly a convent, but the women dedicated their lives to God. There were a lot of Beguinages throughout Europe, starting in around the twelfth century, she said, and sometimes they were attached to parishes and sometimes not. They often had what is called a "common fund," so what they earned was put in for all to share.

Elizabeth was not sure she understood what her mother was talking about. Why would the ladies all live in what looked like a little private neighborhood around a square, instead of in one building like the sisters who taught at St. Joseph's School at home in Westchester?

As they walked among the paintings, Meg explained to Elizabeth about where Auntie Marie lived. "Auntie Marie lives in an abbey, which is like a convent where the sisters who teach you live, because they all live in the same building, but it is also like a little neighborhood where the Beguines lived, because it has a lot of buildings." Meg continued, "It is like a little town, because it has its own church and cemetery, and it is also like a farm, because it has cows and sheep and flowers and a stream out behind the buildings."

That only confused Elizabeth more. She wondered how a convent could be a town and a farm all in one. She listened, a little distracted by the paintings and the sculpture. They drove back to the B&B (Uncle Jimmy had to go back to work on his ship) and as soon as she got into the back seat, Elizabeth fell asleep.

CHAPTER EIGHT

The next day, Elizabeth and Meg took a funny flat ferry across to Cobh and saw the immigration museum there and the big cathedral that had a resident cat sitting on the altar rail, ignoring all the visitors.

While they were walking around the cathedral, Meg told Elizabeth that on Friday they would drive out to Magarry in West Cork to see Meg's sister Marie. Elizabeth's Auntie Marie was now the abbess of St. Joseph's Abbey there.

Meg told Elizabeth about how they grew up together, with Uncle Jimmy, and both girls went to South Presentation Convent in Cork (Uncle Jimmy went to the Christian Brothers on the Rochestown Road). Meg told Elizabeth how Auntie Marie was the smartest of the three of them, how she got all "A"s in school and even won the Latin contest when she was Elizabeth's age.

That sounded a little daunting to Elizabeth. She had never studied Latin, and her grades were OK, but not that great. But, on the other hand, Auntie Marie sounded a lot like St. Brigid. At least, Elizabeth thought, Auntie Marie was Irish, and she ran an abbey. Elizabeth wondered if Auntie Marie could turn water into beer.

On Friday, Uncle Jimmy came to the B&B around 9:30 in the morning. Elizabeth was as dressed up as she could be—she was, after all, on vacation—but this seemed to be a very important day. She would be meeting her Auntie Marie for the first time, *and* she would be meeting a real, live abbess, just like St. Brigid.

They got in the car. Uncle Jimmy drove and Meg sat in the front, and they headed west toward Magarry. Elizabeth sat by herself in the back seat, wondering all along about what she would say, and what Auntie Marie would say, and if she would like her Aunt, and what the abbey looked like. She still could not get her mind around what her mother told her the other day when they saw the painting of the Beguinage in that art gallery in Cork City. How was an abbey like a town and a convent and a farm, all at the same time?

They drove out through Douglas, and over past Cork Airport, and through some little villages. Meg marveled at how much the west side of Cork City had grown. Before Elizabeth knew it, they were on a small, windy road out in the countryside. Then they came upon a place with hedgerows and a big gate. There was a sign that read "Saint Joseph's Abbey – Cistercian – Please use next drive for all deliveries."

Elizabeth took a deep breath. "Whew," she thought. "Here we are."

They rang the bell and then drove through the opened gate and up a very, very long driveway. Elizabeth saw cows on one side of the drive and a funny tall grass on the other. A big black and white dog followed alongside the car for a little while, barking.

"That's called a Border Collie," said Uncle Jimmy. "They can grow to be almost two feet high. This one's a pup."

Now Elizabeth was totally confused. It was a town and a convent and a farm, and they had a dog, too?

CHAPTER NINE

They stopped by the front door of St. Joseph's Abbey. There were lovely flowers, all red and yellow and purple, with big green leaves, in big urns on either side of the door. They rang the bell, and a young nun answered and, before they said a word, she said, "Welcome! Mother Marie is expecting you. Come in."

They followed the nun to a little parlor on the right, just inside the door. There were more flowers on a big round table, like a coffee table, with four lovely wooden high-backed armchairs around it. The room was very bright and airy, with big windows that overlooked the front drive. There was a big crucifix over the door. Elizabeth looked around. "Those must be pictures of saints or something," she thought. The only ones she recognized were the one of St. Joseph holding the baby Jesus and a pretty, white flower, and another of Jesus's mother, Mary.

Suddenly, a tall nun appeared at the door. They all turned. It was Marie! She went to Jimmy and they hugged and laughed, and then Marie went to Meg and they hugged and laughed and cried. So far, no one had said a word. It was just laughing and crying and hugging. Then Meg turned Marie around to face Elizabeth.

"Elizabeth," Meg said, "this is your Auntie Marie." Elizabeth put out her hand, and she and Marie shared a proper handshake.

Elizabeth was terrified. She did not say anything, she just looked up at her aunt. Later, Elizabeth remembered that

Auntie Marie said something like, "I am very pleased to meet you, Elizabeth. Your mother has told me all about you in letters and emails."

"Emails?" Elizabeth thought "Abbesses can turn water into beer and they also use email?"

Before they knew it, the young nun who answered the door came back holding a tray with cups and saucers and a teapot. They all sat down around the big coffee table, and Auntie Marie poured them each a cup of tea.

Meg and Uncle Jimmy and Auntie Marie laughed some more and shared the news of cousins and neighbors and schoolmates from years past. Then Uncle Jimmy looked at his watch and said he had to go over to work, but he would come by later to bring Meg and Elizabeth back to their B&B.

The convent parlor was bright and airy, with big windows overlooking a lovely rose garden. A bird sang nearby, but Elizabeth could not see it. Meg and Auntie Marie were catching up. It had been such a long time since they saw each other, but Elizabeth knew they were on the telephone every so often, although not as often as you would think for two sisters.

Marie looked at Elizabeth. Her eyes were blue as the ocean, like Meg's and Nancy's and Bill Jr's and Elizabeth's.

Marie brought Elizabeth into the conversation. "So, Elizabeth, how has your trip been so far?"

Elizabeth sat up straight (after all, Auntie Marie *was* an abbess) and said: "Oh, Auntie Marie, I have had just the best time. We flew to Shannon Airport in the biggest plane ever, and we went to Cobh, and we went to the art gallery in Cork, and..." Elizabeth was almost out of breath.

Auntie Marie and Meg laughed softly, as Elizabeth continued her list of where she went and what she did and when she did it.

It was almost time for prayers, so they finished their tea and Auntie Marie brought them into the abbey chapel and showed them to seats behind a little railing (it looked like the altar rail at an old church Elizabeth once visited), and Auntie Marie disappeared through a door in the main chapel.

CHAPTER TEN

The abbey chapel was long and narrow, with a very high ceiling. It was plain, but very pretty. There were two rows of raised seats running up and down the left and right walls, and there was a long, raised stand in front of each row of seats that looked like a music stand. There were big books opened in front of every seat. There was a long open space in the middle of the chapel, empty except for a big square altar and a very large candle on a stand.

At one end there were three high windows that looked out to the hills. Elizabeth and Meg sat in the front row of seats at the other end, facing the windows, behind the little railing. There were three more rows behind them, but they were the only people there. There were little booklets that someone had marked to the day and the time. Elizabeth read the big black letters: "TERCE."

Soon, a door on the left opened and Auntie Marie appeared. She pulled a long cord just next to the door, and a little bell rang, just once. Auntie Marie was followed by other nuns, old and young, short and tall, thin and not so thin. They walked silently in single file, following Auntie Marie, until she crossed over to the right side and stood at a place in front of a big, high-backed chair at the end of the second row. The nuns took their places in the high benches on either side of the chapel. One of the nuns sat by the organ and began to play, and suddenly

Elizabeth heard the most beautiful singing she had ever heard in her life.

There must have been twenty or twenty-five nuns, all standing at their places with big books open before them. Auntie Marie sang first: "God, come to my assistance," and all the nuns sang, "Lord, make haste to help me." Then they all sang, "Glory be to the Father and to the Son and to the Holy Spirit, as it was in the beginning, is now, and ever shall be, world without end. Amen."

Auntie Marie had the most beautiful voice. She sang the beginning line of the psalm printed in Elizabeth's little booklet, "Upon all who do my will, I shall pour my spirit," and then the nuns sang together the rest of the psalm, first one side, then the other. They sang in English, and Elizabeth followed in her little booklet: "I call, and he answers me," and "I lift my eyes to the mountains." Then Auntie Marie stood and read something—it sounded like something from the Bible—and then they sat quietly for a few minutes. (That part was not in Elizabeth's booklet.)

Next, Auntie Marie stood, and they all stood, and then she said: "Let us praise the Lord," and then they all said, "And give him thanks."

And then Elizabeth saw the most astonishing thing. Auntie Marie said, "May the Lord bless you, in the name of the Father and of the Son and of the Holy Spirit," and while she said the blessing, she made the sign of the cross, just like the priest does at the end of Mass.

It was over in about five minutes, maybe seven, thought Elizabeth. The sisters left the chapel by the same door they came in, one by one, following Auntie Marie.

Two minutes later, Auntie Marie appeared again, this time from another door behind Meg and Elizabeth, and came into their section behind the little railing.

That was when Elizabeth noticed Auntie Marie was wearing running shoes!

"Elizabeth," said Auntie Marie, "your mother had a very good friend in school, Janie, who became a Cistercian just like me here at this abbey. Janie is now very ill, and I am going to take your Mum to the infirmary so they can have a little visit. Would you wait right here for me? When I come back, I will take you around the abbey."

Elizabeth nodded, taking in the entire situation. She was in a Cistercian abbey in Ireland where she had an aunt who was an abbess who used email and who wore running shoes.

CHAPTER ELEVEN

The chapel was quiet. Elizabeth sat, waiting for Auntie Marie, and saw a big rope to her right, against the wall. The floor was a shiny, gray stone, and the walls were a dull, tan stone. It was an ordinary day for late April in Ireland, except the sun was out and the colored glass at the end of the chapel made a pretty pattern on the floor.

Auntie Marie came into the chapel through the same door she and the other nuns left by. Elizabeth stood up. (They always said at school to stand when a sister entered the room. Elizabeth was not sure whether aunts counted, but she figured it couldn't hurt.)

"Now, Elizabeth," said Auntie Marie, "I propose we visit around the abbey. We have just an hour until Midday Prayer and dinner. Your Mum is upstairs with Sister Jane, who has been very ill. Come along, now."

Auntie Marie opened the little gate on the railing and motioned to Elizabeth to come through, into the chapel itself. They walked over toward the big square altar in the middle of the open space, closer to the railed off area where Elizabeth and Meg sat during prayers, about equal the distance between there and where the nuns' benches started along the walls.

"This," said Auntie Marie, touching the big square stone table, "is the altar the priest says Mass upon. Come around this side."

They stood, now facing the section where Elizabeth and Meg sat. Auntie Marie pushed the white cloth covering the stone back a little and pointed to a shiny small square of marble, with a cross on it, set into the stone. "Here is where the relic is."

"Relic?" Elizabeth wondered what a relic was. She looked up at Auntie Marie, but she did not say anything.

Auntie Marie continued. "The priest stands here when he says Mass. There is an old tradition," she continued, "that priests face east, toward the rising sun, when they say Mass. Mass begins after Lauds, our Morning Prayer. We pray Lauds up in our stalls, like you saw us just now, and then for Mass we gather around the altar."

Now Elizabeth had heard everything. At St. Joseph's School the sisters never went near the altar during Mass. Sometimes she would see old Sister Lawrence up there, changing the candles and fixing the flowers and cleaning up a bit after Mass, but the only people near the altar when the priest said Mass were the priest and sometimes another priest or even the new deacon in the parish. They did have altar servers at St. Joseph's School Masses, usually boys from the eighth grade and lately some of the eighth-grade girls, but never, ever did Elizabeth see women standing around the altar during Mass.

Auntie Marie noticed the look on Elizabeth's face, and asked, "Have you never seen women at the altar, Elizabeth?" Elizabeth shook her head.

Auntie Marie said, "Well, there are some superstitions about women and girls being near the altar at any time, let alone during the Mass. In the very early Church," Auntie Marie continued, "there were women called deacons who did what all the other deacons did during the Mass. No matter where they were, the men of the Church complained about them. In the fifth century, Pope Gelasius complained that women were at the altar 'doing what men do.' Of course, we do not know exactly what he complained about...."

Elizabeth stood, wide-eyed. Women at the altar? Like, deacons standing next to the priest while he said Mass? Like Auntie Marie and the other nuns, who stood around the altar when the priest said Mass? Her jaw dropped a little and she stared at her aunt, then followed her as she led Elizabeth to the chapel's side door.

CHAPTER TWELVE

Elizabeth caught up with her aunt. Meanwhile, Auntie Marie continued speaking about women deacons as they headed toward the door. "Yes, Elizabeth, historians tell us that women served the priest at the altar, in different times and in different places. Many of these women were ordained as deacons." Auntie Marie opened the door and they went through. The door opened to a long hallway that had the most polished floors Elizabeth had ever seen.

"Many of these women were ordained as deacons," Auntie Marie repeated, "but they were not exactly like the deacons we have today. On the other hand, they were not that different."

Down the hall, they came upon a large room, like a library, with books and tables and very large windows. "This," Auntie Marie said, "is the scriptorium. At least that is what we call it. In the Middle Ages, monasteries had rooms where the monks would write and copy and decorate manuscripts. They made psalter books, like the ones you saw in our chapel. You had a small section of the book when you prayed Terce with us."

Elizabeth gathered her courage to ask a question. "Auntie Marie," she said, "did nuns in abbeys write manuscripts too?"

"Why, certainly!" Auntie Marie replied. "Did you ever hear of Hildegard of Bingen?"

Elizabeth shook her head, "no."

"Well," Auntie Marie said, "Hildegard of Bingen was born in Germany at the end of the eleventh century, and she lived to be more than eighty years old. She was a very special woman. No one knows exactly when she went to the Benedictine monastery in the forest, in a place called Disibodenberg. Some say, when she was about eight years old, her parents sent her to live with a woman named Jutta, who cared for her and taught her to read Latin and that, after six years, they both professed vows as nuns. So, I guess, technically, Hildegard became a nun when she was fourteen years old."

Elizabeth blinked. Fourteen! Just two years older than Elizabeth was now. And Hildegard studied Latin!

"Auntie Marie," Elizabeth asked, "what did Hildegard do at the monastery when she was such a little girl?"

Auntie Marie smiled. "Well, Elizabeth, that is the problem of all the history about women in the Church. No one knows exactly what they did." Elizabeth watched Auntie Marie look out the window; she seemed to be staring off into space.

"But does anyone know anything?" Elizabeth asked. "I mean, does anyone know anything about the history of women in the Church?"

Auntie Marie turned toward Elizabeth. "Yes," she said. "Many people know a lot. But many people do not want to believe the truth about the history of women in the Church."

Auntie Marie sounded a little upset, and Elizabeth worried she had made her aunt angry.

Auntie Marie continued. "Remember how I told you about Pope Gelasius in the fifth century, and about how he was upset that women—I happen to think they were ordained women deacons—about how he was so upset that women were serving at the altar 'doing what men do'?"

"Yes," Elizabeth answered.

"Well, by the time Hildegard entered the monastery at Disibodenberg in the eleventh century, most of the Church tradition of ordaining women as deacons had faded away."

Now Auntie Marie was going too fast. She said that women did what the men did and she said they were ordained, and now she was saying they were not ordained anymore.

"Was Hildegard ordained, Auntie Marie?" Elizabeth asked.

"That's an interesting question," Auntie Marie said. "Let's go over to the bakery and see the nuns making altar breads."

CHAPTER THIRTEEN

Elizabeth did not want to upset Auntie Marie, and she really did want to see what else was happening inside the monastery, so she did not press the question. Even so, it turned and turned in her mind: Was Hildegard ordained?

Sister Nicholas opened the door to the bakery. "Good morning, Mother Marie!" Sister Nicholas said cheerfully. "This must be Elizabeth," she said.

Sister Nicholas was tall and, well, she just looked jolly. She was wearing a giant white apron over her habit, and her veil was pinned back, and her sleeves were pushed up. And she kept talking.

"Elizabeth," she said, "welcome to the bakery!" Sister Nicholas smiled and continued, "Or, at least, welcome to part of the bakery. Here is where we make the altar breads for the priest to use at Mass. These big machines are called 'Wafer Baking Machines,' but you can see they are really like big waffle irons. We mix flour and water to get a paste and then place a scoop of the mixture and then press down the top of the machine and then turn it on and then when they are done the light goes off and then we use the cutter to trim the edges and then we put them onto onion skin paper and into this rack over here called a humidifier and then after a day we take them out and separate the onion skin paper from the giant cooked wafers and then put a big stack of them over here to this machine and here, let me show you...."

"Thank you, Sister Nicholas," said Auntie Marie. Elizabeth was trying not to giggle. Sister Nicholas was very interesting, but Elizabeth wondered how she talked so much without taking a breath.

They went over to another big machine where another nun was using a big punch to go through a stack of the giant cooked wafers. Then they walked to a table where blue plastic tubs of wafers sat (Auntie Marie whispered that they were left there to finish drying) and then they saw the locker with the wafers in big plastic jars. Auntie Marie said there were 500 wafers in each jar.

They turned and went out the door they came in, passing Sister Nicholas, who was busy working the giant baking machines. Auntie Marie nodded and Sister Nicholas nodded back.

Elizabeth thought that rather strange but did not say anything.

As they walked down the big corridor, Elizabeth asked Auntie Marie again: "Was Hildegard ordained?"

"Hmm," Auntie Marie replied. "That is a very good question. You see," she continued, "Hildegard was an abbess."

"Like you, Auntie Marie?" Elizabeth asked.

"Yes, Elizabeth. Hildegard was an abbess, like me. But in the eleventh century, the church still ordained women as deacons. Sometimes abbesses were ordained as deacons as well as consecrated as abbesses."

"What does 'consecrated' mean, Auntie Marie?"

"Well," Auntie Marie began, "consecrated has a number of meanings. Like many words, it is used in different ways for different things. For example, when the priest says Mass, he consecrates the hosts, the wafers you saw in our bakery. The wafers become the Body and Blood of Jesus."

"Yes," said Elizabeth, "Sister used that word at St. Joseph's when we were preparing for our first communion."

They came upon another door, which Auntie Marie opened, and soon they were in another workshop. This one looked like a greeting card factory, which indeed is what it was.

CHAPTER FOURTEEN

The room was big and bright, and two sisters were in it, at the two ends of the room. There were greeting cards all over the room. There were cards in slots and cards on tables and cards in boxes, all neatly arranged. One sister was at a computer, and the other sister was boxing cards.

They greeted Elizabeth and Auntie Marie, who introduced them as Sister Agnes and Sister Kathryn. "Sisters," said Auntie Marie, "this is my niece, Elizabeth." Each sister smiled and greeted Elizabeth, but did not say much, if anything. Auntie Marie explained that the monastery earned its keep in different ways: They sold altar breads (the communion wafers in Sister Nicholas's bakery) to parishes and convents across Ireland. They sold greeting cards they designed and printed at their little shop and by mail. They even had a CD of the nuns singing Christmas music for sale.

"Come," Auntie Marie said to Elizabeth, "we should not disturb the sisters."

That was something Elizabeth began to notice. The nuns at Auntie Marie's abbey did not seem to talk that much.

As they went down the hall, Elizabeth asked again about Hildegard.

"Hildegard is a doctor of the Church," said Auntie Marie, "but she did not have an easy time of it. When she was elected to lead her community of nuns, to be the '*magistra*,' the abbot of the territory disapproved. He wanted to call her something else: prioress. You see, in different places in Europe the women who led abbeys were the equivalent of bishops. They had what is called 'territorial jurisdiction' over everything that happened in their territories."

"Was that like being the governor?" asked Elizabeth.

"Well, not quite," answered Auntie Marie, "but it was close. You see, there were abbeys and monasteries, usually what are called royal abbeys and royal monasteries. They were in many countries, certainly in France, Italy, Spain, and Sweden. For seven or eight centuries after their founding, from around the time of Hildegard until the late nineteenth century, the abbesses of these abbeys and monasteries ruled completely."

"Was Hildegard one of them, Auntie Marie?"

"Well, she could have been, but she had so many disagreements with the local abbot that she and her sisters moved to another village. She kept her authority inside her buildings, but she did not oversee the lands around her. That meant she was more like a mother superior and less like a bishop."

"What about the nuns in France and Italy and Spain and...?" Elizabeth could not remember the other country Auntie Marie mentioned.

"And Sweden," Auntie Marie replied. "Well, the abbesses of many of the abbeys and monasteries there had what is called 'ecclesiastical jurisdiction,' which meant they had the same authority as bishops. They were the ones who appointed priests and allowed them to hear confessions and celebrate Masses in their territories. They were the ones who managed Church legal proceedings."

Elizabeth looked up at her aunt. "Are you that kind of abbess, Auntie Marie?"

"No, Elizabeth," Auntie Marie said. "Pope Pius IX ended all that in 1873. He wrote what is called a 'papal bull,' titled 'Differences' and that was that."

Elizabeth thought she heard Auntie Marie sigh as they turned the corner to the back door.

CHAPTER FIFTEEN

The abbey garden was amazing. Elizabeth followed Auntie Marie out the door and could not decide where to look first. There were so many flowers, every color and shape she had ever seen and many she had never seen. Auntie Marie began to say the names of some of them, as they walked the small path between the rows.

There were bluebells and buttercups, and daisies and violets, and (it seemed in a special place) orchids of every color Elizabeth could name.

"In April," Auntie Marie began, "some very lovely flowers stand up straight and tall, so we cut them to put by the altar. "See the gladiolus, over there?" Auntie Marie pointed to a tall plant with bell-shaped flowers. "It is one of the flowers we cut in April. Of course, we try to have white lilies for Easter, and we grow them over in the greenhouse."

Auntie Marie pointed to a funny little glass-walled building at the end of the garden. As they looked inside, Elizabeth felt the moisture and smelled the fertilizer that brought all this color from the ground.

"Eew," Elizabeth said. "What is that smell?"

Auntie Marie laughed softly. "Elizabeth," she said, "we run a farm here at the abbey. We have cows and sheep and chickens. They make some very good fertilizer for the flowers."

Elizabeth did not ask anything else. She figured out what the smell was.

As they walked along the rows, Auntie Marie again began to speak about Hildegard of Bingen.

"Hildegard knew everything about plants, especially herbs and spices. She wrote a big book about what to use for different sicknesses." Auntie Marie stooped to pick a gray-green leaf from a plant and gave it to Elizabeth. "This is sage. Hildegard recommended sage tea for just about everything."

"Were there more abbesses like Hildegard?" Elizabeth asked.

"Yes, very many," said Auntie Marie. "We do not know all their names, or where they lived, because over the centuries many of their abbeys were taken over by governments or, sometimes, by the local bishops."

"How could that happen?" Elizabeth asked.

"Well, convents and monasteries and abbeys are supposed to be separate from dioceses," Auntie Marie began. Elizabeth noticed a slight change in her voice. "And," she continued, "sometimes when the nuns became too old, or even when they were not, they were 'asked' by the local bishop to move. And sometimes, whether they moved on their own or not, their buildings fell into ruin and their records were lost."

Elizabeth picked a small shiny leaf from a big bush and smelled it. "What is this?" she asked.

"That is rosemary. We use it when we cook chicken, which is not very often. I don't know if Hildegard said it would cure anything, but it does taste good."

"Why don't you eat chicken a lot?" asked Elizabeth.

"Well," Auntie Marie said slowly, as she stepped carefully near the chicken coop. "We Cistercians are mostly what today the world calls 'vegetarians.' We really don't eat meat, and we eat very little fish or chicken, although every abbey has its own way of interpreting the Rule of Benedict."

They walked near the chickens and Auntie Marie continued, "These little ladies give us eggs."

The chickens scratched and clucked. Some ran toward them and some ran away. Auntie Marie looked at the scrambling chickens and said, half aloud and half to herself, "How like things in the Church."

CHAPTER SIXTEEN

Elizabeth was not sure if she was supposed to hear what Auntie Marie said so softly it sounded as if she was sighing. She did think Auntie Marie's comment a little strange. The Church is like a bunch of chickens making noise and running in many different directions?

But, Elizabeth wanted to know more about the abbesses like Hildegard. When they got near the lambs in their pen, Elizabeth asked, "Auntie Marie, can you tell me about other abbesses besides Hildegard?"

Auntie Marie bent over and petted the most adorable little lamb. It licked Auntie Marie's hand and, Elizabeth thought, winked at her.

"Elizabeth," Auntie Marie said, "we don't know everything about the abbesses of history. As I told you, many of their abbeys and monasteries died out, and the buildings either fell into disrepair or the local bishops took them over. Perhaps on the way home, Uncle Jimmy will ride you past Kilcrea Friary. It was not a women's monastery, and the site is mostly ruined now, but it will give you an idea of what I mean."

Elizabeth thought it a funny name, "Kilcrea."

Auntie Marie continued, "Kilcrea is the English for *Cill Chré*, which is Irish for the Cell of Cyra, or St. Cyra. 'Cell' is the monastic name for the little room where we sleep."

ELIZABETH VISITS THE ABBEY

They walked along the road toward the cows. Auntie Marie continued, "St. Cyra was the sixth century abbess who founded an abbey for nuns near the town of Ovens, here in County Cork. There is nothing left of her abbey today, but near it, in the fifteenth century, Franciscan friars founded Kilcrea Friary."

"Who was St. Cyra?" Elizabeth asked.

"That's the problem," Auntie Marie said. "We do not know much about her, except she is a saint, her feast day is October 16, and in the sixth century she founded a monastery near here."

"That is all we know?" asked Elizabeth, wide-eyed.

"Yes, Elizabeth. There is scholarship about early abbesses and prioresses, and there are a few stories about Saint Cyra." Auntie Marie continued, "But many of the records of abbeys and monasteries have been lost. So, we do not know exactly who did what in the early centuries of the Church, even here in Ireland."

"But were there other abbesses in Ireland before you, Auntie Marie?" asked Elizabeth.

"Oh, yes, of course," Auntie Marie chuckled. "Not far from here, over in Ballyvourney, there was an abbey that lasted from the seventh until the twelfth century. There were nuns in Cork City and also over in Youghal in the thirteenth century, until they were run out in the middle of the sixteenth century when the British king at the time, Henry the Eighth, broke from the Catholic Church."

The names and places swirled in Elizabeth's mind. She had heard of Youghal. It was on the seacoast and Uncle Jimmy told a story about it one night by the fire just the other day, but Elizabeth could not remember it. She had fallen asleep before it ended.

They walked along the fence near the cows, big black and white cows out in the fields. The cows ignored them, and

Elizabeth just put one foot on the split-rail fence and looked in. Auntie Marie stood silently next to her.

Elizabeth looked up. "Auntie Marie," she asked, "when did abbesses begin in the Church?"

CHAPTER
SEVENTEEN

Steel-gray clouds began to gather in the sky, and in a moment the sun was gone. As they walked, a little wind came up and Elizabeth watched the yellow flowers along the fence start to dance.

"That is called gorse," Auntie Marie said, noticing how Elizabeth watched the flowers dip and bow in the wind. "You can make a tea with it that might smell a little like coconut. My father, your grandfather, told me that when he was a boy on the farm, they would soak the seeds in water and wash the dog with it. He said it kept the fleas away."

They turned a bend in the road and the abbey church was straight ahead.

"But you wanted to know about abbesses," Auntie Marie said. "Well, we should begin many centuries ago, even before the time of Hildegard, but also in Europe. We need to go back to the sixth century, to a place called Arles in Gaul, what we now call France. There was a bishop, now a saint, called Caesarius of Arles. He was a famous preacher, and he supported monastic life."

The rain began to fall. Then it stopped, and the sun broke through.

"Caesarius wrote a book with a Latin name, *Regula virginum*. Most people today call it *A Rule for Nuns*."

"Like you?" Elizabeth asked.

"Yes," Auntie Marie smiled, "Like me. There is a technical difference between 'nuns' and 'sisters.' Nuns live in cloisters, like this abbey; sisters make what are called simple vows, and live in convents in cities and towns and sometimes in the countryside. Sisters are more likely to be teachers or nurses or parish workers, while the vocation for nuns is to pray."

Auntie Marie continued, "Caesarius's sister, I think her name was Caesaria, headed a small group of women dedicated to a life of prayer. Caesarius built a monastery for them."

"Why would he do that?" Elizabeth asked.

"Well," Auntie Marie continued, "we will never know all the details, but there seem to have been many groups of women who wanted to live as the monks did, devoting their lives to prayer. But we know of only a few women's monasteries as compared to those of the men."

Elizabeth looked up at her aunt as they neared the abbey. "Why?"

"That is both a big and a small question, Elizabeth." Auntie Marie's voice seemed to change a little. "You see, in many places of the world, even in Europe, women were not treated very well. There was even a movement that asked if women were the same species as men, or maybe women were something else."

"Species?" Elizabeth asked.

Auntie Marie chuckled, "You will learn all about 'species' when you get to secondary school, I think around ninth grade in the United States. 'Species' means living beings exactly the same, even though they have different attributes."

By now, Elizabeth was totally confused. But she hung in there.

Auntie Marie continued, "All human beings are exactly the same, but different. You know that. Some are tall and some are short, some are left-handed, and some are right-handed. Some have different color skin than we. And some are male and some are female."

That part Elizabeth understood. Her mother explained it to her.

"But Auntie Marie," she asked, "what difference do the differences make? We learned in catechism class that all are made in the image and likeness of God. The teacher said it did not matter if someone was tall or short, or had a different colored skin, or was a boy or a girl. She said we were all human."

"Exactly," Auntie Marie said, as she opened the door to the abbey church, and they both went inside.

CHAPTER EIGHTEEN

It was time for prayers again. Elizabeth went to the little section in the back and sat next to her mother, who was already there. Meg handed Elizabeth the little booklet, and suddenly Auntie Marie appeared through a side door to the chapel with all the nuns filing in after her, one by one.

They took their seats, and Auntie Marie chanted: "O God, come to our assistance," and the nuns chanted, "O Lord, make haste to help us."

The prayer seemed to be the same as at ten o'clock, but a little longer. There were three psalms, a short Scripture reading, a prayer, and the blessing. Auntie Marie chanted the blessing, and the nuns closed their books and followed her out the same door they came in. It was about 12:30 in the afternoon.

Quick as lightning, Auntie Marie was in the guest section of the chapel with Elizabeth and Meg.

"Come," she said. "It's time for dinner."

The guest dining room in the abbey was small and simple. The table was set for three, and Meg and Elizabeth sat while Auntie Marie disappeared. In no time, Auntie Marie and another nun brought trays with plates piled high with food. There was ham and cabbage and carrots and potatoes and a light gravy and little bread rolls and butter. There were water glasses on the table, and Auntie Marie's tray had a pitcher of water.

"Well," said Meg, once they were settled and had said grace. "How was your morning, Elizabeth?"

Elizabeth already had a mouthful of food. She swallowed and began to tell her mother all about the places she had seen in the abbey. She told her about the place they make the altar breads, and funny Sister Nicholas, and where they make the greeting cards. She spoke about the garden and the herbs and the roses and Hildegard of 'Binging.'

Auntie Marie laughed and said, "It's Bingen, not 'binging,' Elizabeth."

Elizabeth got a little red in the face, but that did not stop her from listing everything she could remember about Hildegard and her herbs, and the chickens and the eggs and the lambs and the cows.

Auntie Marie turned to Meg, saying, "I told her about the early monasteries for nuns in Ireland and Europe."

Meg said, "Good. We don't know enough about the women of the Church, let alone the early women."

"Here in the monastery, we study our own history," Auntie Marie said. "We have so many books in our library that no one of us would ever be able to read them all. We study Scripture, for sure. But we read history."

Elizabeth watched as the two sisters leaned a little closer. Meg looked at Marie and asked, "Do you think it will ever change?"

"Who knows?" answered Marie. "The men are in charge."

"But Auntie Marie, you were telling me about the bishop in France who helped the women," Elizabeth said.

"Yes," said Auntie Marie. Looking at Meg, she continued, "There was a very powerful bishop, Caesarius of Arles, and his writing is one of the earliest examples of a common rule, as we call it, for women. What he wrote is like the Rule of Benedict that we Cistercians follow."

The conversation drifted away from the history of women in the Church to Janie—Sister Jane—who Meg visited in the infirmary, and to talk about other schoolmates of Marie and Meg. It was ordinary conversation between two sisters who had not seen each other in a long time, and who would not be seeing each other again for a while, either.

CHAPTER NINETEEN

The midday dinner finished, Auntie Marie disappeared again, first with one tray and then with the other. Elizabeth and Meg brushed off the table and put the butter in the little refrigerator near the sink.

Auntie Marie came back and sat at the table. The abbey was very quiet, but it seemed to be quieter. Auntie Marie said, "Now we have free time here. Some sisters take a nap, some attend to their personal sewing or email, some read the newspaper or a magazine."

Meg looked at her watch. Uncle Jimmy would be coming soon. She turned to Elizabeth and asked, "Is there anything else you want to ask Auntie Marie?"

Elizabeth said, "Would you finish the story about the Bishop of Arles you began when we were near the cows?"

"Of course," she said, "let's bring your mother up to speed." So, Auntie Marie recounted how Caesarius of Arles was an important and powerful bishop whose sister gathered a group of women for whom he built a monastery.

"To put this all into context," Auntie Marie continued, "we need to understand two things: first, there were women in the early church ordained as deacons and, second, Caesarius was such an important bishop, he was allowed to have deacons. Remember, up until the time of Hildegard, many abbesses were both consecrated as abbesses and ordained as deacons."

Elizabeth knew about deacons. There was one in her parish, Mr. O'Flaherty, who used to be the sixth-grade teacher at St. Joseph's School until he retired about a year ago. Elizabeth remembered going to the funeral of her friend Sara's grandfather, and Mr. O'Flaherty was there all dressed up almost like a priest, helping the priest at Mass and even reading the Gospel.

"We do not know if Bishop Caesarius ordained women as deacons—there were local laws in Gaul, or France, that repeatedly outlawed ordaining women deacons from the end of the fourth until the middle of the sixth century—but we do know that Bishop Caesarius built a monastery for women who wanted to live a life of prayer and possibly service as best they could."

Auntie Marie continued, "Also in Europe in the sixth century, there was a woman named Radegund. She was a princess, and she gave a lot of money to the poor. But she wanted to live a life of prayer and service. She told Bishop Medard that if he would ordain her a deacon, she would build a monastery to care for ill people. In short: He did, she did, and Radegund is remembered as a saint to this day. She and her sisters followed Caesarius's *Rule for Nuns*."

Earlier, Elizabeth must have been distracted by the excitement of seeing the nuns' bakery. Now, the information finally sunk in.

"Do you mean," Elizabeth asked wide-eyed, "that there were ordained women deacons in the early Church?"

"Oh, yes," said Auntie Marie. "Have they not taught you that at school?"

CHAPTER TWENTY

The doorbell rang. "That must be Jimmy," Meg said to no one in particular. Elizabeth seemed to be staring off into space. Auntie Marie stood up and went out of the kitchen to the guest entrance door.

Jimmy threw his arms around Auntie Marie and said, "How are you doing, Sis?"

Elizabeth overheard them laughing and chatting in the hall. She was happy to know that Auntie Marie's brother could still call her "Sis," even though they were both grownups now and Auntie Marie, after all, was an abbess of this huge abbey.

Jimmy and Auntie Marie came into the kitchen. There were more hugs and kisses all around. They all seemed both happy and sad at the same time.

"Will you have a cup?" Auntie Marie asked Jimmy. Just then, Meg remembered bringing tea to Bill in the Shelbourne Hotel all those years ago. She half chuckled to herself, remembering how it spilled.

"I'd love one," said Uncle Jimmy, "but I can't. I've just the time to get Meg and Elizabeth back to Cork and then I have to go back to work for a bit. I'll come and see you myself soon," he said.

The brother and sisters stood very close together, and Meg reached out to Elizabeth to enclose her in a group hug. Elizabeth thought she saw her mother begin to cry.

"Please, God, it won't be so long before we are all together again," said Auntie Marie. They squeezed a little closer, and then they hugged and kissed each other, and then they stood apart and just looked at each other. Not one of them wanted to move.

"Freeze the moment," said Meg, using an expression she picked up in New York.

They walked slowly to the door, Meg and Auntie Marie arm in arm, and Elizabeth and Uncle Jimmy following.

Goodbyes are hard, and this one was especially hard for Meg, who had not seen her big sister in so many years and was not likely to see her soon again. Uncle Jimmy's car was right there. Elizabeth turned to Auntie Marie and gave her another hug, and Auntie Marie bent close to her ear and whispered: "Don't forget about women deacons."

They hugged and then Elizabeth got into the back seat of Uncle Jimmy's little car. She watched as Uncle Jimmy kissed Auntie Marie on the cheek and got into the driver's seat. Then, she watched as Meg and Auntie Marie shared a long hug.

They drove down the road away from the abbey, and Elizabeth saw Auntie Marie give one last wave before she disappeared behind the guest door entrance.

When they were on the main road, Elizabeth asked if they could drive past Kilcrea Friary, the place Auntie Marie told her about. She was pretty sure it was on the way back.

"Of course," said Uncle Jimmy. "We can't stop for long, but I know right where it is, near Ovens. Why do you want to see Kilcrea?" he asked.

"Oh," Elizabeth said, "Auntie Marie told me the best stories about nuns and monks in Europe in the sixth century, and she said there was a nun who lived near there and that is how it got its name."

"You're joking," said Uncle Jimmy. "It's an old friary, where monks lived. I went there on a school trip when I was your age. There were never any nuns there."

"Maybe no and maybe so," said Elizabeth, very sure of her facts. "Auntie Marie said there was a nun called St. Cyra who built a convent near there in the sixth century and her feast day is October 16." Elizabeth was quite sure of her facts, even though they were the only facts she had. Uncle Jimmy did not say anything.

CHAPTER TWENTY-ONE

They took the turn out the abbey drive and headed toward the main road. Before she knew it, they were at the Kilcrea Friary ruins. The site was bigger than Elizabeth thought. They stopped and walked around.

There were big stone arches around a graveyard that had big gravestones with Celtic crosses. There was a railed off stone box and the sign said it was the crypt of Arthur O'Leary, who seemed to be some sort of lord of the manor or something. The ruins of the church stood tall, without a roof or windows or doors. There was a little map of the friary on a wall, and Elizabeth marveled at how much it was like Auntie Marie's abbey, with a kitchen and a chapter room and places to work and to eat and to study, all connected to the church. The difference seemed to be that the rooms surrounded the friary garden, while Auntie Marie's abbey had the garden out the back door.

Kilcrea Friary was a quiet, dreamy sort of place. Elizabeth looked up at the surprisingly blue sky and wondered why there was nothing about St. Cyra there.

"Let's be off," said Uncle Jimmy. He was looking at his watch, and Elizabeth was worried she would make him late for work. Meg sat in the front, and Elizabeth had the back seat all to herself.

It did not take long to get back on the Cork road. They passed the airport, which was fun, because they were up on a hill and

ELIZABETH VISITS THE ABBEY

could see the city ahead. Before she knew it, Elizabeth was looking at the door to their B&B.

"I'll be off," said Uncle Jimmy. Meg and Elizabeth went inside.

Once upstairs, Meg asked Elizabeth, "So, how did you like your day at Auntie Marie's abbey?"

"I loved it!" Elizabeth exclaimed. She retold what Auntie Marie said about the nuns and abbesses of history, and especially how some of them were ordained deacons like Mr. O'Flaherty, who used to be the sixth-grade teacher at her school.

"And your Auntie Marie told you there could be women deacons in the Church today, I suppose," Meg said a little skeptically.

"Well, I don't know," Elizabeth answered. "She did say that there were definitely women ordained as deacons in the past and she talked about a nun in the sixth century named Radegund who definitely was ordained."

Meg stood and looked out the window as a tanker made its way out toward the sea.

Elizabeth continued, "There was another nun Auntie Marie mentioned, I think she was named Caesaria. Her brother was a bishop and started a monastery for her and her friends. I cannot remember if she was a deacon."

"Nobody can," thought Meg to herself. She turned to Elizabeth and asked, "So, what do you think of all this? What do you think about women in the Church?"

That was a very big question. Elizabeth looked at her mother and said, "I don't think we know as much about them as we do about the men."

Meg smiled, thinking, "How right you are." Meg was not especially what people call a feminist, but she knew full well that today's Church was not that much different from the Church in the sixth century. Of course, Radegund was ordained a deacon, and probably Caesaria was, too. And Meg knew there were hundreds, probably thousands more women deacons, but the records were lost or, more likely, destroyed.

"You're right," Meg said. "Let's get ready for when Dad comes home."

CHAPTER TWENTY-TWO

Their final days in Ireland flew by. They all went up to see Uncle Jimmy's ship, LÉ *Ciara*. He said it was a Peacock-class patrol vessel stationed right there in Haulbowline, and he had five officers and thirty-three enlisted men working for him on it.

As the four of them—Uncle Jimmy, Meg, Bill, and Elizabeth—went around the ship, everybody saluted Uncle Jimmy and called him "sir."

"Are you like Auntie Marie?" Elizabeth asked.

"What do you mean?" Uncle Jimmy laughed.

"Are you in charge of the ship, like Auntie Marie is in charge of the abbey?" she asked.

"I guess you could say so," Uncle Jimmy mused. "I am the abbot of *Ciara*," he laughed. "But you know, Elizabeth," Jimmy looked at her intently, "there was a real St. Ciara up Tipperary way. She was born in the seventh century. Come here, see the plaque."

Elizabeth and Jimmy went into the officers' dining room, with Meg and Bill close behind. There, on the wall, was the story of St. Ciara. The plaque said she was a nun in Kilkeary, near Nenagh in Tipperary, who founded a convent. Then she founded another monastery in Cork, where she remained until her death in 679.

"Uncle Jimmy," Elizabeth asked wide-eyed. "Is your ship named for the nun who lived near Kilcrea Friary?"

"Well, yes it is," Jimmy laughed. "I'd forgotten to tell you that when we were out there. The poor girl had so many names—some people called her Cere or Ciara or Cera or Cyra. But here we call her Ciara, and we depend on her a little to get us through the storms."

"I thought she was a sixth-century nun?" asked Elizabeth.

"Well, that's the problem," said Uncle Jimmy. "She was for sure around that time, and as I know the story, she and five other women began an abbey up in Nenagh, as I said. Then, at some point, she came to Cork and founded another abbey out by Ovens, where we were the other day. Or, she was two people."

"I do not understand," said Elizabeth.

"Well," said Uncle Jimmy, "there are not very good records of women in the early Church here in Ireland. Your Auntie Marie must have told you that." He stepped past a big rope and helped Elizabeth get past it.

"We just do not know whether the nun in Tipperary and the nun here in Cork were the same person," Uncle Jimmy continued. "We only know that she was an abbess, or they were abbesses."

"If she was an abbess, was she a deacon?" Elizabeth asked.

"We do not know," Uncle Jimmy sighed. "We only know the stories, the legends, and the little bits of written evidence here and there in manuscript libraries here in Ireland."

"Do you think abbesses were ordained deacons, Uncle Jimmy?" asked Elizabeth.

"Of course, they were," he said.

Meg and Bill stood a bit apart from Elizabeth and Jimmy, watching and listening to their conversation. Meg wondered what Elizabeth would bring back to her class at St. Joseph's in Westchester County. The pastor was not fond of the topic of women deacons, she knew. Her women's group tried to have a speaker come to talk about her new book and the pastor did not allow it. He said something like, "Of course, we are very interested in the roles of women in the Church, but women, of course, cannot be ordained and, of course, you understand."

"Of course," Meg had said dryly.

CHAPTER TWENTY-THREE

The road from Cork to Shannon Airport was so different from when Meg and Bill had been in Ireland years before, and so much different from the way it was when Meg was a little girl. Now, it was mostly a straight highway and they flew past the farms and small villages beyond the road.

Their final few days in Cork packed in a frantic round of visits to friends and relatives, up in the city, down in Monkstown, over at Roches Point. Elizabeth followed their journeys on the fold-out map Uncle Jimmy bought her. Now, she was tracing the highway up to Shannon.

They stopped near a town called Hospital. Elizabeth thought that a funny name for a town, but the sign was right there. When they came out of a little shop, Elizabeth saw a clump of yellow flowers near the walkway. "Auntie Marie said they are called 'gorse,'" she said, "and that your father used it to make tea."

"Yes," Meg chuckled, "bruise the flowers a bit, mind the little bugs, put two tablespoons full into boiling water, let it steep, add a little honey. It's good for what ails you."

Jimmy and Bill were at the gas pump—they call it petrol in Ireland—and once they finished, the four of them got back into the car for the last bit of the journey to Shannon Airport, about twenty-five miles from the town called Hospital.

Soon enough, the sign "Welcome to Shannon Airport" appeared before them. Uncle Jimmy pulled the car into short-term parking right in front of the big glass terminal building, unloaded their luggage, and before she knew it, Elizabeth was on the escalator toward the security check and US Customs area. It all happened so fast!

Uncle Jimmy went as far as he could with them. In the old days, he might have been able to walk them right to the gate, but no longer. Bill and Jimmy shook hands, Meg and Jimmy hugged, Uncle Jimmy bent and gave Elizabeth a little kiss on the cheek. And then they parted.

After they checked their bags, they went through security and followed the signs to "US Citizens," where there were actual Customs and Immigration Officers from the United States who checked their passports and asked if they had been on a farm or were carrying any food or "monetary instruments valued at over $10,000." Elizabeth was glad her parents were answering for her; she wasn't sure what a "monetary instrument" was, but if it was a check she knew she did not have one. She was not sure if Auntie Marie's monastery counted as a farm, so she tugged at her mother's jacket and whispered in her ear.

Meg said to Elizabeth, "Ask the man."

So, Elizabeth said, "I was at my Auntie Marie's monastery and we walked near the chickens and saw a lamb and then we saw the cows and before that there were so many flowers...." The Customs Officer interrupted her, "So, Miss, did you happen to collect any eggs, or touch a cow or lamb or anything else at your Auntie's monastery?"

"No," Elizabeth said firmly, "I did not."

"Well, fine then. And welcome to the United States," he said.

That, of course, totally confused Elizabeth, who knew for sure they were still in Ireland, in Shannon Airport, and they had not even gotten near the plane yet.

CHAPTER TWENTY-FOUR

The plane was as big as the one they came to Ireland on, but Elizabeth was able to see more of it in the daylight. It was very, very big.

Elizabeth could see through the big windows in the boarding area, where they were waiting, that it was painted green on top and a silvery-white on the bottom. And she could see it had a name, *St. Mella*. Elizabeth thought that an odd name. She had never heard it before, and she wondered if it was the name of a man or a lady.

When they went inside the plane, Elizabeth remembered more about her trip from Kennedy Airport to Shannon. The seats were arranged the same way and they were the same color and had the same little pillows and blankets on them.

Soon enough, the captain's voice came over the speakers—in Irish and English—and then the flight attendants were demonstrating how the seatbelts worked and telling the passengers what to do in an emergency. Elizabeth took the emergency instruction card from the seatback pocket and followed along.

They started to take off and, as they went down the runway, Elizabeth saw a magpie, then another, then a third. Meg, seated next to Elizabeth, saw them as well and smiled softly.

"Elizabeth," Meg said as the plane took to the air, "you know there are a couple of sayings about magpies in Ireland. One is that if you see one before you depart, you will be back again."

ELIZABETH VISITS THE ABBEY

"Oh, I hope so," said Elizabeth. "I so want to visit Auntie Marie again and hear more about the history of women in the church."

"Yes," said Meg, "that would be good."

They flew over the coast. Meg told Elizabeth that the rocks and surf beneath them were called the Cliffs of Moher, and soon they were above the clouds. A good dinner came next: chicken and vegetables and potatoes and a bit of cheese and some crackers wrapped in plastic. After the meal, the flight attendants brought ice cream! There were little video screens at each seatback, and Elizabeth could choose any one of about a hundred movies. (She could not see all of them because Meg put "parental controls" onto Elizabeth's screen.)

Elizabeth started a movie. She had already seen *Frozen* in the movie theater back home in Westchester, but she thought it would be fun to see it again. But, soon enough, she was asleep. It was not that late in the day, but the excitement of early rising and the drive and the busy-ness of the airport combined to make her drowsy.

What began as a short nap soon turned into a real sleep, as Bill and Meg and Elizabeth sped west toward New York. Elizabeth was clearly in dreamland, and Bill and Meg dozed a little too.

They landed at Kennedy Airport right on time. It was still light, but even though she had a little snooze, Elizabeth felt like it was the middle of the night, which of course it was by now in Ireland. They went straight out to get their luggage and were in a share-ride van going home before they knew it. That was the advantage of US Customs and Immigration at Shannon.

Once in her own bed, Elizabeth fell into a deep sleep, half remembering the dream she had on the airplane. She thought she might talk with her mother about it in the morning.

CHAPTER TWENTY-FIVE

Elizabeth woke up very early the next day; her body seemed to think she was still in Ireland. She stayed in bed as long as she could, but finally went down to the kitchen, where Meg and Bill had already nearly finished their breakfast.

Elizabeth wanted to tell her mother about her dream, but she was not sure she wanted to share it with her father. Strange as it may seem, that night she had the same dream she had when they were on the plane to New York.

Elizabeth did, however, want to know who St. Mella was. It was such an odd name, she thought, and probably the name of someone very important. After all, it was a very big plane. Her father had his tablet right there at the table, so she asked him to look up St. Mella.

"Where did you come up with that name?" Bill asked, looking over his coffee cup.

"It is the name painted on the side of the *Aer Lingus* plane we took home from Shannon to Kennedy," Elizabeth reported precisely.

"Well," Bill said, apparently somewhat bemused. "St. Mella was an abbess. It says here she was an eighth-century abbess in County Leitrim. That is up north," he said.

Elizabeth was fascinated. Another abbess.

"Does it say anything else about her?" she asked.

"Yes," Bill smiled. "It says she ruled her abbey and its territories as if she were a bishop."

Meg looked over at the drawing of St. Mella. "Look, Elizabeth," she said. "Here is St. Mella with a bishop's crozier. Sometimes they call it a bishop's crook." Meg remembered there was a bishop's crozier in the Hunt Museum in Limerick, at least the top part of it.

Bill gave the tablet to Elizabeth.

Elizabeth stared at the drawing. It seemed to be an icon, which would make sense, given that St. Mella, the Abbess Mella, was a saint. And she was holding a shepherd's crook, like the one Auntie Marie showed her next to the big chair in the abbey chapter room. She asked her father about the crook.

"It is a sign of authority," Bill explained. "The bishop carries it as a sign of his authority over a diocese. It seems abbesses carried them, or at least had them, as signs of authority over their abbeys, or maybe even over their abbey lands."

That reminded Elizabeth of what her aunt told her: The abbesses in a lot of European abbeys and monasteries had authority. Elizabeth thought she remembered Auntie Marie calling their authority "ecclesiastical jurisdiction," and that they were like bishops. She definitely remembered about how they lost that kind of authority, even over their own abbey territories. She could not remember the name of the pope, but she did remember it happened with a document with a very funny name, a "papal bull." Elizabeth did not like that. She also wondered why her Auntie Marie was not a deacon.

CHAPTER TWENTY-SIX

few days later, Elizabeth went to school. She told her friends all about her trip to Ireland to see her Auntie Marie and her Uncle Jimmy.

Everyone was interested to learn about Ireland and the plane rides and Uncle Jimmy's ship. They asked a lot of questions about Auntie Marie and the abbey, and they were surprised when they heard all the stories about how abbesses were once like bishops. They were more surprised when they learned that abbesses (and many other women) were ordained as deacons.

What do you think? What do you think about women in the Church?